Rita and Rascal

Autum Agusta

Order this book online at www.trafford.com
or email orders@trafford.com

Most Trafford titles are also available at major online book retailers.

Printed in the United States of America.

ISBN: 978-1-4669-6971-1 (sc)
ISBN: 978-1-4669-6973-5 (hc)
ISBN: 978-1-4669-6972-8 (e)

Library of Congress Control Number: 2012921944

Trafford rev. 01/04/2013

 www.trafford.com

North America & international
toll-free: 1 888 232 4444 (USA & Canada)
phone: 250 383 6864 ♦ fax: 812 355 4082

Table of Contents

Chapter I

Coon Hunting

"Cool!" Danny exclaimed. "Did you just say that your grandpa wants you to go out to his place on the creek and try to find a baby raccoon for a pet? With an unusual pet like that I could be as important as my big brother that is a football hero!"

"Grandpa said those critters get into his garden and pull up his vegetables. He said he would like to get rid of them and this is the time of the year for the babies to be born," Alan explained.

"My mom is at the school lunchroom fixing food for the sports banquet tonight. Since the high-school teams won three championships this year, it will be a big event. I will have to go by there and ask her if I can go coon hunting with you," Danny said.

The two twelve year old boys jumped on their bikes and rushed to the lunchroom.

Rita looked up from a pile of pealed potatoes when her slender, freckled-faced, redheaded son came running through the door. "Before I say yes, how far is it to your grandpa's farm, how will you get there, and when will you be back?" she asked.

"It is only six miles, we will ride our bikes, and we won't be gone very long," Alan answered.

"If you aren't back by dark I'll come looking for you," Rita said.

It's awful hot so let's stop by my place and get some water before we leave town," Alan said.

The boys were putting water containers on their bikes while Alan's mother fixed two juicy peanut-butter and jelly sandwiches for the boys. She also put in some cookies and apples into the sacks to complete the meal. Mrs. Willie handed the sacks to the important hunters.

Danny followed Alan through town and onto a dirt road leading north to the creek. They came to the first creek two miles from town. Parking their bikes on the only hill for miles, the boys ate their lunch. "Please let us find a baby raccoon," they prayed before they ate.

The country was starting to turn green after a cold winter, but the boys were too excited to notice. All they could think about was having a raccoon for a pet.

"I wonder what kind of animal that hawk is searching for over there?" Danny asked, pointing his finger west.

"I don't know, but maybe we can keep a baby coon from becoming some big bird's meal," Alan answered.

Thirty minutes later Alan and Danny saw the creek where grandpa lived.

"Are you going to go to your grandpa's house first?" Danny asked.

"No, he will want us to stay and visit and we just don't time," Alan said with a feeling of importance.

The boys hid their bikes in some bushes not far from the road. They motioned to each other to be quiet, and tip-toed through the tall, dry grass to the creek. Their exciting hunt had begun.

The creek was not running but there were several water holes in the lowest places. The boys started their hunt on the east side of the bridge. They walked around the first water hole. Sure enough, there were two different kinds of tracks. One set of tracks looked like a rabbit's hind foot and the tracks that went with them looked like a baby's tiny hand prints.

Yep, there in coons around here all right," Alan whispered.

The tracks seem to lead to nowhere. The boys decided that the animals went over some hard ground that didn't make foot prints. Alan pointed to the west side of the bridge. Danny shook his head to agree.

"There are more trees and water on that side," Danny whispered.

The boys found more coon tracks and tip-toed around every water hole. They were as quiet as the animals around them.

Alan pointed to a huge rock. "Let's crawl up there and look on the other side," he whispered.

Alan and Danny climbed the huge rock and looked over the edge. Underneath the high side of the rock was a porky pine digging in the dirt. The boys shook their heads "No" and quietly crawled back down.

The young hunters felt disappointed as they searched more areas of the creek, and didn't find any wild animals except for the tiny minnows in the water.

It's time to head back," Alan said. "Maybe it is too early for the coon babies to be born," he sighed.

Danny agreed. As they were walking back to the place they had left their bikes, he said, "I'm going to look in that old tree stump over there before we leave."

"Aw, it's too close to the ground and too close to the road. I'm sure no coon would be dumb enough to have her babies in there," Alan said.

"Well, I'm going to have a look anyway," Danny said as he quietly walked toward the old tree stump.

•   •   •

Chapter II

The Find

Danny quietly walked toward the tree stump. He could vision a fierce tiger coming through the tall dry grass toward him. He shuttered and put one foot on a bare root of the old tree and the other foot on what had been a low branch. Danny pulled himself up even with the top of the stump. The inside was much deeper than it looked on the outside. The bottom was covered with dry leaves. Danny slid both feet down the inside of the old tree. "I hope the bottom isn't too deep and nothing very wild is in here," Danny whispered to himself. He felt his feet hit the bottom and balanced his body and turned loose.

Running his hands through the dusty, brittle leaves from last summer, Danny touched something wet and warm. He jerked his had back. Something was hidden in the leaves. Danny

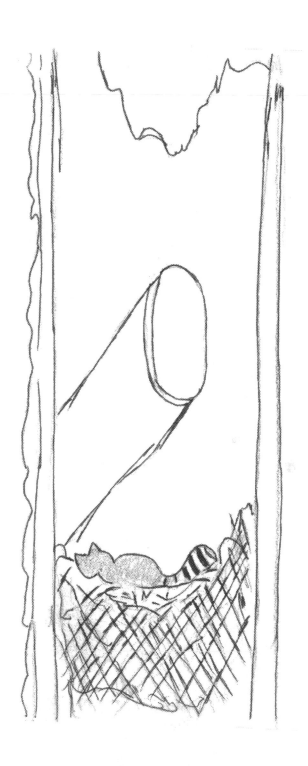

carefully parted the leaves to see what he had touched. "It's probably some kind of a large insect," he told himself.

It was no an insect. Lying in the loose leaves was some kind of tiny animal. It was long, gray and alive. The animal looked kind of like a picture of a weasel Danny had seen in a book at school. The tiny animal's eyes were still closed so tightly that it was hard to tell where they were supposed to be.

"I found something but I'm not sure what it is!" Danny yelled to Alan.

The boys were too excited to be quiet now.

Alan slid down in the tree stump with Danny. "It must be a raccoon, but it doesn't look like one," Alan said. "The ones I've seen have black rings around their tales and black masks around their eyes that make them look like bandits."

"Whatever it is, there is only one, and there are two of us," Danny reminded Alan.

Alan ran his fingers through the leaves until he was convinced that no more tiny animals were in there. "Let's not get this one yet but look for another one before we leave," Alan said.

"No. The mother might come back and get this one while we are gone. I'm going to take him with me right now!" Danny exclaimed. He took off his shirt and pulled his undershirt off over his head. Danny put his other shirt back on and then gently picked up the wet, newborn baby and wrapped him up in his undershirt. He handed the baby to Alan. "Just hold him while I get out of here and then you can give him back to me while you crawl out," Danny said.

Danny tried to keep the baby warm by holding him under his shirt next to his own warm body. It was too late to look for another baby and the boys needed to start back to town. "The baby is getting cold and we need to hurry home," Danny said. He wrapped the baby tightly in his shirt and put him in the basket on his bike.

The sun was quickly going down and a cold wind was blowing. Two miles later Danny stopped his bike and put the baby next to his own body again. He tied his outer shirt at the bottom to keep the baby from falling out. Although they rode their bikes as fast as possible, it was almost dark when they reached the lunchroom.

Danny ran into the lunchroom. "Look what I found, mom!" he shouted.

"I was about ready to come looking for you. Well, let me see what you found," Rita replied. She reached for Danny's bundle and carefully opened the undershirt and looked at the strange creature. ""Son, I'm afraid you found a weasel not a raccoon," she said.

"I don't care what he is," Danny replied. "He's cute, isn't he," he asked.

"I guess," Rita answered. "Is this all you found?" she asked.

"Yes," Alan answered.

"The baby's head is so small and his mouth so large," Rita said. "And, do you know what else?" she asked.

"No what?" the boys asked.

"Do you know why he is wet?" Rita asked. "He had just been born when you boys came along and scared the mother. She ran away before more babies were born. She didn't even have time to give him his first bath," She explained. "It's a wonder he is still alive," "How are you going to feed something this tiny?" Danny's mother asked.

I hadn't thought about that," Danny answered.

"I better get home before my folks come looking for me," said Alan.

"I'm through working here for awhile. Let's take the car to Alan's house. It will be faster and maybe the baby won't get any colder," Rita said.

Danny and Alan jumped into the back seat of the Brown's car and Rita hurried across town to Alan's house. Danny kept the baby close to his body. The weather was feeling more like winter than spring now. The wind was blowing harder.

Mrs. Willie stopped fixing supper long enough to look at the new baby. "Mom, do you think he is a raccoon?" Alan asked.

"He is too young to tell for sure," Alan's mother said as she looked at Danny's prize.

"Mom, do think L.C. will let the baby get his dinner with her kittens?" Alan asked.

All we can do is try and see," Mrs. Willie answered. "We call our mother cat L.C. because her name is Lazy Cat," she explained.

Alan put the baby into the box with L.C. and her six kittens. Baby felt the warm fur of the mother cat and smelled her warm

milk. He was so excited and hungry that he made a terrible screaming noise. "Screech, scratch!" squealed Baby.

The terrible noise scared L.C. right out of her box. She jumped high in the air and landed a foot away from the box. L.C. stood frozen on the floor with her fur standing straight up on her back. Her claws were sticking out in all direction. She was not going to get back into the box as long as that wild creature was in there.

"Well, it looks like you blew that dinner," Danny said. He lifted the baby out of the box and held him tight. "Now what are we doing to do?" he asked.

"Mrs. Willie, you wouldn't happen to have a doll bottle around your house anywhere, would you?" Rita asked.

"It has been so long since my three girls were small enough to play with dolls. I don't think we have anything like that around anymore," Mrs. Willie answered. "I'll look anyway," she said. Mrs. Willie returned a few minutes later. "I'm sorry, but I can't find any type of a small bottle," she said.

"We might have an old baby bottle around our house but I think it would be too large for the baby's tiny mouth. We'll just have to try it and see," said Rita. She started home and left the boys off at the lunch room to pick up their bikes while she hurried home with the baby.

Rita laid the bundled baby on the kitchen cabinet. By the time she found the old baby bottle, the two boys were riding their bikes into the driveway.

Alan and Danny watched Rita clean the bottle. She filled it half full of milk from the refrigerator and finished filling it with hot water. This made a warm watery liquid.

Danny held his new pet like a real baby and tried to put the bottles nipple into the tiny mouth. Everyone was surprised when the tiny mouth opened wide enough to get a good hold on the nipple. Baby was soon getting his tiny belly full of food.

"I think he's going to make it with an appetite like that," Rita said with a grin.

"Yeah!" Danny and Alan shouted

Chapter III

Taking Care of Baby

After Danny's pet was full and asleep, Alan helped Danny fill a box with rags. The baby was put in the box and Danny placed the box next to his bed.

"You will have to feed him about every four hours," Rita told her son.

"I will have to set my alarm clock to do that," Danny replied. He set the alarm clock next to his bed to ring in four hours.

"I need to go home," Alan said.

"Would you like to come back later this evening?" Rita asked. "Mr. Brown and I are going to the athletic banquet tonight. You can come over and spend the evening with Danny, if you want," she said.

"Sure! I can help Danny take care of Baby!" Alan exclaimed.

Alan had just left when Danny heard his father drive up to the house. He was coming home from work.

"Look what I found today," Danny said. He led Ray Brown into his bedroom and parted the rags to show off his new pet. "What kind of animal do you think he is, Dad?" Danny asked.

"I have no idea, son, but I know it will take a lot of work to keep a baby that tiny alive," Ray Brown answered.

Danny shivered to think that maybe Baby would not make it or live long enough to grow up. "Please keep Baby alive Lord," he prayed.

While the Browns were at the Banquet that night, Alan and Danny spent the evening just watching the baby sleep. They didn't even take time to watch TV.

When the alarm sounded, Danny filled the baby bottle with cold milk and hot water just like his mother had done. He held Baby in his arms and pushed the nipple in the tiny animal's mouth.

Baby nursed almost all the milk without completely waking up.

"You are a good mother," Alan said, laughing.

Ray and Rita Brown came home at 10:30. Rita took Alan home and Danny set his alarm to ring again at 2:30 the next morning. He laid Baby in the box and petted him before he crawled into his own bed.

The alarm rang. Danny crawled out of bed and fixed Baby another bottle. Baby's tiny paws clutched the bottle. Danny thought that he could hear Baby purring like a kitten. He was so sleepy that he wasn't sure that was the sound that Baby was making.

It seemed to take Baby a long time to nurse all the milk. Danny even fell off to sleep a few times while feeding Baby and he was glad to see the bottle empty. He put baby in the box and was asleep as soon as his head hit the pillow. Danny woke up and sat up in bed. He had forgotten to set the alarm for Baby's next feeding. If he missed one feeding, Baby might die. "Oh Lord, help me not to forget again," prayed Danny.

Danny set the alarm to ring again at 6:30.

The alarm sounded. Danny felt sleepy as he fixed Baby's next meal. He heard his father getting up to go to work.

"It looks like you are taking good care of your new pet, son," Ray Brown said when he came through the kitchen. He watched the tiny animal for a few minutes. "He sure is an unusual looking animal," Danny's father said. "It will be interesting to see what kind of animal he is, if he makes it." "I'll see you tonight," Ray Brown said as he left the house to go to the local café for coffee and visiting with friends.

When Baby finally finished his bottle, it was too late for Danny to get any more sleep. He went to the bathroom and started to get ready for school. His mother had cereal on the table for Danny and his brother Ronny when Danny came out of the bathroom. The boys ate their breakfast while Rita got ready for work.

Rita Brown taught one of the sixth grade classes and she taught her son Social Studies and Math.

"Mom, could you feed Baby for me at noon while I'm at school?" Danny asked.

"Sure. One of the other teachers has playground duty today," Rita answered. "I can hurry home and feed him before I teach my afternoon classes, but when I have playground duty, you will have to hurry home and feed him." "Are you going to always call him Baby?" she asked.

"I'll have to call him Baby until he gets old enough to tell whether he is a raccoon or not, and then I can give him a proper name," Danny answered.

Ronny was old enough to drive his own car to school and work. "I wish I was old enough to drive to school, but I do have the most special pet in town anyway," Danny told himself. He felt real cool as he crawled out of his mother's car.

Rita let Danny out close to the playground so he could play with his friends before the morning bell rang. She parked the car in the area for teacher parking and hurried to her classroom and to prepare for a busy day.

Danny waited until the teacher and all the students were seated in the classroom before he made his announcement. "I have a new pet. It is a tiny baby, and we think it is a raccoon or a weasel. It is too small to tell for sure. I had to get up twice last night to give it its bottle. I have decided to call him Baby until he gets older, and then I can give him a good raccoon or weasel name," he told his class proudly.

"May we see your new pet when he is old enough to bring to school?" Mrs. Conley asked.

"Yes, mam," Danny replied as he sit down in his desk. He felt important.

Rita walked her students to the lunch room then hurried home to feed Baby. She held the tiny animal on her lap with one hand and held Baby's bottle with the other hand. Rita was surprised that Baby was strong enough to hold onto the bottle. He soon emptied the bottle, and Rita hurried back to school to teach her afternoon classes.

Danny rode home with his mother that evening instead of walking with his friend in order to feed Baby sooner.

Rita cleaned house and started supper. Danny fed Baby, and then went outside to shoot baskets in the back yard with some friends. He soon came back into the house. All of his friends were following him. The kids all went into Danny's bedroom where everyone took turns petting the sleeping baby in the box.

"I wish I had a pet like that!" Rita heard several children say. She also heard Danny say, "They are a lot of work, and will cause you to lose a lot of sleep."

During supper that night, Danny said, "Mom, I told the kids at school that I have a new pet, and they want me to bring it to school when it is old enough." "Is that all right with you, Mom?" he asked.

"It's all right with me if it's all right with your other teachers," Rita answered.

On Friday evening Danny and Alan were jumping on the trampoline in the back yard. Rita heard the boys coming into the house. "Alan wants me to go back to the creek with him tomorrow and find him a pet like mine," Danny said.

"If the weather is as warm tomorrow and it has been today, you may go with him," Rita answered.

The next morning was warm. Danny fed Baby, ate his breakfast and was putting on his jacket when Alan rode into the driveway on his bike.

I fixed some lunch for you guys today," Rita said. She handed Danny two brown paper bags.

Danny looked inside. There were bologna and cheese sandwiches, potato chips, bananas, brownies, and a can of pop in each sack.

"Yum, yum. Thanks," both boys said.

Rita wished the boys good hunting and waved good-bye. She watched Alan and Danny make a circle with their bikes on the driveway and paddle down the street. This was her day to wash and iron clothes, clean house, wash the car, and to do a little yard work. Rita was so busy with her work that she forgot that the baby was in the box in the bedroom. She was glad that Danny had set his alarm clock to remind her to feed the new house creature. They could not take a chance to miss one his Baby's feedings.

After forty-five minutes of hard pedaling Alan and Danny reached the creek. This time they went to talk to Alan's grandpa. "Grandpa, we only found one baby animal on the creek last week. We want to find another one this week," Alan explained. "Do you have any idea where we can look along the creek?" Alan asked.

"I have a feeling that they build their nest pretty close to my garden," Grandpa answered with a frown. "The big raccoons come into my garden and eat most of my corn crop and many other vegetables. They are very healthy animals. I think the young ones must be pretty close by." "They always make their nest in a hollow tree to protect their babies from danger. I wish you could catch all of them so I wouldn't have to worry about my garden," Grandpa said with a chuckle.

"Thanks grandpa. We better get started hunting if we expect to find another baby animal," Alan said.

The boys looked everywhere they had looked before. Alan and Danny crawled into the old tree stump again and searched through the dead leaves several times. They were hoping that the mother had returned to have more babies. The more they looked, the more disappointed Alan felt.

It was still early in the day. The boys had time to look a long way down the creek on the east side of the bridge behind grandpa's house.

"Look at that old tree over there," Danny whispered. He pointed toward a very tall cottonwood that was dead at the top. The top looked like it might be hollow like the one where they had found Baby.

"I think we should climb up there and look inside," Alan said.

"I don't know if we should or not. It looks awfully high," Danny replied.

Danny climbed to the first branch and lay across it. He reached down for Alan's hand and helped him up.

Danny let Alan climb up on his shoulders in order to each the next branch. Alan lay across that branch and reached down for Danny's hand. Some of the branches were close together and easy to climb. Other branches were so far apart that the boys almost fell while reaching for each other. If the top of the tree had been any smaller around, it would not have been strong enough to hold the boys. The last branches crackled with their weight.

Alan let out a sound of disappointment when they reached the tree top. There was no hollow part or place for a raccoon nest. "I guess we went to all this trouble for nothing," he said with a sigh.

"I guess so, but look how far we can see from way up here," Danny replied.

Alan looked around in each direction. "Yeah," he said.

The boys saw the dry creek winding its way across the otherwise flat land. The grandparent's house and farm buildings looked like toys. The bridge to the west looked like a toy train bridge. "There is no way we can ever search over this whole creek," Alan said.

Danny agreed. "I hope it will be easier to get down than it was to climb up here," he said.

The boys climbed down from the tall cottonwood tree a little faster than they had climbed up. There were still some scary places where they almost fell to the ground far below and prayed for safety.

Danny scratched his arm against the tree trunk while he was helping Alan down from a branch. Alan twisted his leg when he almost missed a branch with his foot. They were scraped, scratched, tired, and disappointed by the time they were safely on the ground.

Alan and Danny searched a little further. The trees seemed to be getting smaller, and the water holes further apart. "I think we need to go back to town and look again next Saturday on the west side of the bridge," Danny said.

Alan did not answer. He quietly followed Danny back to where they had left their bikes hidden in the bushes.

The boys had been so busy hunting they had forgotten about their lunches. They took the paper sacks out of the baskets on the front of their bikes. Danny followed Alan to a large water hole next to the east side of the bridge. They sat down on the large rocks that jutted out over the water and tossed stones into the water while they ate.

They prayed that they might find another baby.

"At least we can scare the fish," Alan said, tossing and rock into the water.

Alan and Danny searched the creek the next Saturday. They looked on the west side of the bridge and looked a lot further down the creek. The boys had more bumps and bruises while climbing trees and over rocks. It was fun to eat their lunches out on the creek, but there seemed to be no fresh raccoon tracks around the water holes. The boys went back to the farmhouse to talk to Alan's grandpa again.

The raccoons must have had their babies way down the creek this year. I'm sure they are all born by now. I guess you will just have to wait until next spring to fine one," grandpa said. "By the time the little fellers get their eyes open, they are just too wild to catch and make them into a pet," he explained.

"I'll share my pet with you," said Danny.

"I guess that's better than nothing," Alan replied.

The boys said good-bye to Alan's grandparents. They rode their bikes back to town for the last time that spring. It was time for summer baseball season and they would be busy playing ball for most of the summer.

Baby was still sleeping most of the time. He made several strange noises. Baby purred while he was nursing his bottle. Sometimes Rita Brown would forget they had a tiny wild animal in the house until she heard his cooing noise telling her that he was hungry. Danny took care of Baby when he was at home and Rita took care of Baby when Danny was at the baseball field or working for his father.

Baby was now two and a half weeks old. His eyes were still tightly shut. Danny was feeding Baby one morning when his mother said, "Son, I think that Baby's mother left him to die in the nest because she sensed that he was going to be blind."

"I hope not!" Danny exclaimed. He laughed at the idea, but when Baby was three weeks old Danny begin to worry

Rita telephoned everyone she knew that might know something about baby animals. "How old are baby animals when they open their eyes?" she asked everyone.

"They are always open by the time the animal is two weeks old," everyone said.

"Oh dear . . . what are we going to do with a blind pet?" Rita asked herself and Danny.

Every morning Danny jumped out of bed. He gently lifted Baby out of the box and looked at the animals' small head. Baby was now over three weeks old. His eyes were still tightly shut. "I'll love you even if you are blind," Danny told Baby.

On Sunday morning Danny lifted Baby out of the box. He squealed when he saw two tiny shiny eyes staring back at him. "Thank you God that Baby is not blind," Danny said. "Mom . . . Dad . . . Ronny!" Danny yelled. "Baby can see! Baby can see!" he shouted.

The Brown family came running into Danny's bedroom. "He sure looks different with eyes," Ronny said. The others agreed.

"Well, we know Baby can see, but he still has a long gray body. We still can't tell what kind of animal he is," Danny explained.

Alan came over that afternoon to see how Baby looked with eyes.

"Doesn't Baby look different?" Danny asked.

Alan laughed. "He sure does," he answered. "Are you going to call him Baby forever?" Alan asked. "You need to give him a proper name instead of Baby," he said.

"I can't name him until I know what kind of animal he is," Danny explained again. "Certain animals have certain names."

The day Baby opened his eyes he also crawled out of the box. It seemed like every day he made a new noise.

Sometimes he sounded like a cat meowing. Sometimes he sounded like a dog barking. Sometimes he sounded like a bird. Once he even howled like a wolf and coyote.

Baby's strange noises scared the little poodle, Velvet, and she usually hid under the bed. The noises made the large outside dog, Mickey, bark. Sometimes the neighbor dogs barked and were scared of the tiny animal's strange noises.

"How can anything as tiny as you are make such loud noises?" Danny asked Baby.

Every time anyone walked past Danny's bedroom, they had to put Baby back into his box. The Brown family finally decided they would just have to let Baby crawl all through the house. They were careful when they walked from room to room so they would not step on the sleeping Baby.

One night Danny was in bed asleep. He was dreaming that he had just hit a home run in a baseball game. When he ran across home base, he stubbed his toe. Danny's toe begin to hurt more and more Suddenly, Danny was awake. He opened his eyes. His toe was still hurting. Danny raised his leg up to look at his toe. He found Baby hanging onto his toe and chewing on it.

The next night Danny was sound asleep when Baby crawled up on his bed and pinched his nose. Danny scolded Baby and decided to feed him early. He was hoping that Baby would go back to sleep and he could get more sleep, too.

"Baby keeps biting my toes and pinching my nose at night and I can hardly get any sleep," Danny told the Brown family one morning.

The Brown family laughed. "Maybe you need to get a bigger box for him," Ronny suggested.

Danny went down town after school the next afternoon and brought home the largest box he could find. He put Baby in it that night after his feeding. Early the next morning Baby crawled out of the box. He used his long claws to open Danny's bedroom door. He used his claws to open Ronny's bedroom door.

Ronny was quickly awake. "Ouch!" he yelled. "Baby, turn lose of my toe!"

Danny ran into Ronny's room and picked up Baby from Ronny's bed. "It's not so funny when he is biting your toe, is it?" he asked, laughing.

"He does have pretty sharp teeth," Ronny replied.

The next night, Rita and Ray Brown were awakened by a tiny animal feeling of their faces. "Danny, come in here and get this animal of yours right now!" Danny's father shouted.

"Danny, I'm afraid you are going to have to lock Baby in the laundry room so we can get some sleep tonight," Rita said the next morning.

"But mom, I think he is too little to be by himself at night," Danny replied.

"If he was in the wild, he would be alone while his mother went after food," Rita said. "Besides you will know he is all right when you get up to feed him every four hours during the night."

"Baby looks larger every day when I get home from school," Rita told her family at the supper table one night.

"I think the fur around his eyes is getting darker," Danny's father said.

A week later Baby was getting a dark mask around his eyes and rings of dark fur around hit tail. His tail was getting bushy. "I guess he really is a raccoon," Danny said.

"What are you going to call him" his mother asked.

"I thought about calling him the Lone Ranger because he has a mask like the Lone Ranger I watch on TV. You know the old black and white shows. I even thought about calling him Bandit, but he is so ornery, I think I'll have to call him Rascal. He acts like the raccoon we saw in the movie "Rascal'," Danny answered.

Baby was officially name Rascal and was not called Baby again.

•   •   •

Chapter IV

A Visit to the Mountains

Rita Brown was fixing dinner. She heard a noise behind her. Rita turned around and saw Rascal tumbling into the kitchen. He sat back like a six-month-old baby. Rascal turned his head from one side to the other as he watched Rita working on the cabinet. Suddenly he crawled right up her pant leg, up her shirt, and sit on her shoulders to see what she was doing.

"You are cute, but I better put you down before you get into my family's food," Rita said. She put Rascal back in his large box in Danny's bedroom.

After Rascal's first time of climbing up Rita's clothes, he climbed up Danny's, Ronny's, and Ray Brown's clothes just like they were tree trunks. At first Rascal was tiny enough to climb up a person, but as he grew, he almost pulled the person over by his weight. The Brown family noticed that their clothes were getting snags in them. Rascal finally grew too large to climb up anyone although he would try occasionally.

Rascal tried to do everything he saw the Brown family do. His back feet were like a rabbit's, but his front feet were almost like human hands. Rascal picked up and handled objects just like people persons. He tried to write with a pencil and eat with a spoon.

Rascal still needed lots of sleep. His favorite place to sleep was in one of the round trash cans that Rita kept in each bathroom next to the stool.

"Always look before you throw trash into the trash cans in the bathrooms. Rascal may be asleep in there and you don't want to throw trash on him," Danny told the rest of the family.

"I think you should take the boys and visit your sister in the mountains during Easter vacation," Ray Brown told Rita and the boys. "You might like to take Rascal with you. I can't get away from my business right now, but the rest of you can go."

"Would you guys like to take Rascal to the mountains and visit Aunt Janie and her family?" Rita asked Ronny and Danny.

"That sounds like fun," Ronny said.

"Yeah," Danny agreed.

Rita called her sister. "Janie we are planning to come and visit you during Ronny and Danny's Easter vacation," she said. "Do you plan to be home then?" Rita asked.

"Sure, come on over," Janie answered, "We'll be home and glad to see you." "Is Ray coming with you?" she asked.

"No, he has to stay home and work, but we would like to bring our pet raccoon," Rita answered. "Is that all right with you?" she asked.

"That should be very interesting; we have never been around a pet raccoon," Janie replied. "I think my girls will enjoy seeing him too."

On Friday morning Rita told Ronny and Danny to pack their suitcases and put them in the trunk of the car before they went to school that morning. "That way we can come home and quickly change into comfortable riding clothes and get started for Aunt Janie's. I want to be as far as we can before dark," she said.

The boys made sure their suitcases were in the trunk before Ronny drove to school and Danny rode with his mother to school.

Danny was waiting in the car as soon as Rita left her classroom in order. When they came into the house, he changed into some loose-fitting jeans from his school clothes. Danny then fixed a couple of bottles with warm milk and put them into the car. Rascal was asleep in the round trash can in the hall bathroom. Danny put the trash can in the middle of the back seat. Rascal did not wake up. Ronny climbed into the back seat on one side of Rascal and Danny sit on the other side of the trash can.

Rita drove for two hours before they entered a city. She stopped the car in front of a Kentucky Fried Chicken place for supper. Rascal was still asleep.

The Browns enjoyed a meal of fried chicken, hush puppies, French fries, and cold slaw. They finished eating and Rita paid the bill and they started walking out of the restaurant. There was a large crowd around their car.

"Oh no . . . I wonder what Rascal is doing now!" Danny exclaimed. He ran to the car. Rascal was still sleeping in the trash can. The people were standing close to the car window watching the baby raccoon sleep.

"Oh, isn't he cute!" one woman said.

"Oh yes. I have never seen a live one before," a man replied.

"He is so little, and he is perfectly marked. Just look at his mask and the rings around his tail," a younger woman remarked.

"Cool! What I wouldn't give to have a pet like that!" a boy exclaimed.

"Me too!" some other kids sighed.

Danny opened the car door. He carefully took the sleeping baby out of the trash can and proudly held him up for everyone to see. Danny carried Rascal around through the crowd so each person could pet him. Rascal woke up and looked at the people and turned his head from side to side. He could not figure out why the people were excited. He was still too sleepy to let anyone bother him.

The people were petting Rascal for the third time. "We need to be going if we are going to make it across the mountain pass before dark," Rita said.

Danny put Rascal back into the trash can. He put the trash can back in the back seat of the car. Rascal rose up out of the trash can to tell the people good-bye. The people were still waving as Rita backed the car away from the curb and drove down the street to the main highway.

Rascal crawled out of the trash can and upon Danny's shoulder. "You sure are popular, Rascal," Danny said.

Rascal was wide awake now. Danny gave him his bottle. Rascal was old enough to hold the bottle by himself now and was not so much trouble to feed. Rascal nursed all his milk and was ready to play.

Ronny and Danny played with Rascal until they were tired, and then both boys went to sleep.

Rita was enjoying the beautiful mountain area. She was a little nervous about the deep canyon and drop off at the edge of the road. Rita new if a car ran over the guard rails, the drop off was several hundred feet into the canyon floor below. She was watching the road carefully when she felt Rascal on her shoulder.

Rascal played with Rita's earring and hair. Suddenly he reached across her face to pinch her nose. "Danny, get your animal before he makes me run off the road!" Rita shouted.

Rascal made a loud laughing kind of noise.

Danny woke up and grabbed Rascal.

"Keep him busy until he goes to sleep, or until we get to Aunt Janie's," Rita ordered.

The boys found a pencil and watched Rascal try to write with it.

Ronny thought he would hold Rascal for awhile. "Ouch. Rascal sure can bite hard!" he exclaimed when he tried to pick up the little raccoon.

"I guess he is old enough to know what he wants to do," Rita said, laughing.

Rascal was restless again.

Danny searched his pockets to find something for Rascal to play with. He gave Rascal his key ring with keys on it. This kept Rascal busy for awhile. Danny gave Rascal his wallet and Rascal enjoyed taking everything out of it. This kept the baby busy for a little longer.

Danny dug some articles out of his suit case and let Rascal play with one of his shirts, his tooth paste, and tooth brush, and his comb. He did not know where to get anything else for Rascal to play with when Rascal grew tired of the things from his suitcase.

"Hey, mom, there is the road leading up the mountain to Aunt Janie's house," Ronny said.

Rita put the car into low gear and drove up the narrow road to Uncle Bill and Aunt Janie's place.

The Browns crawled out of t he car and looked around. In every direction were beautiful ranges of high mountains. They could see a fish hatchery south of them. When the fish are large enough, they are put in the streams for people to fish for them," Rita told Danny and Ronny.

Janie and Bill came out of the house to welcome their company. Kimberly, who was eight-years-old, was following Janie. Kristi, who was five-years-old, was following Kimberly.

Rita hugged Janie and her family. "What is that on your shoulders?" Janie asked Danny.

"I want you to meet my new pet, Rascal Raccoon," Danny said proudly.

"Cool! He is cute!" everyone exclaimed.

"Mommy, I want to hold him," Kimberly said. She started to pull Rascal from Danny's shoulders.

"You better be careful because he bites," Ronny said.

Kimberly pulled Rascal off of Danny's shoulder and hugged him. Rascal was as limber as a rag doll. He snuggled up to Kimberly's cheek.

"Well, I'm surprised at that," Ronny said.

"I want to hold him too," Kristi said. She pulled Rascal out of Kimberly's arms and hugged him. Rascal was still relaxed and limber. Kristi carried him into the house with Rascal's long tail and back legs dragging behind them.

"I guess Rascal knows that the girls are little like him, and he likes their attention," Uncle Bill said.

Everyone watched Rascal explore the living room and kitchen. Janie poured and served hot coffee and hot chocolate. "Are you hungry?" she asked.

"No. We stopped in the city and ate supper," Rita explained.

Rita, Bill, and Janie were talking in the kitchen. Danny and Ronny were in the living room watching TV. They heard Kimberly and Kristi laughing. "Oh no. I wonder what Rascal is into now!" Rita exclaimed.

Everyone ran into the girl's bedroom and started laughing. The girls had put doll clothes on Rascal and were pushing him around in their doll buggy. The girls played "dolls" with Rascal for the rest of the evening.

"You are going to make a sissy out of him," Danny said, laughing. He was glad to have someone help keep Rascal busy.

It was soon time to go to bed. "Where does that animal of yours sleep?" Aunt Janie asked.

"We put him in a box and lock him up in our laundry room at home, but I guess he better sleep with me tonight," Danny answered. "Maybe he is tired enough to sleep all night after he has his bottle."

Kimberly and Kristi took turns feeding Rascal. Danny enjoyed the help. It was almost like a double vacation not having to take care of Rascal all the time. Rascal snuggled between Ronny and Danny and slept all night.

The girls made a doll out of Rascal the next day. Ronny and Danny had time to explore the area around a mountain stream close to Janie's house.

"What is that over there?" Danny asked.

"I'm not sure but I think it might be a beaver pond," Ronny answered.

The boys walked over to the large pond. They saw furry animals scampering back and forth under the water. "They must be working on their burrow," Danny said. "We had a movie about beavers at school."

It wasn't long before the boys heard their mother calling them to dinner from the top of the hill.

After dinner Ronny and Danny walked down to the fish hatchery. There were three large rectangle-shaped ponds. The first pond had tiny trout in it. They were so small that the boys could only see the wiggly tails in the water. The second pond had thousands of fish in it that were about four inches long. The third pond had fish that were over a foot long. Some of them looked like they would weigh as much as five pounds.

"Why are there three ponds with different size of fish in it?" Ronny asked the hatchery owner.

"We have to keep the fish separated so the bigger fish won't eat the smaller fish," the owner said.

"How do you separate thousands of tiny fish?" Danny asked.

We put escape routes from one pond to another. The escape pipes are too small for the larger fish to go through. When the smaller fish's life is in danger, they can always run for cover through the pipe." The man explained.

"I wish I had an escape gate for me to run through when my big brother runs after me," Danny said.

"You can fish for the large ones if you want but it will cost you twenty-five dollars," the owner said.

That sounds like a lot of money, but we will ask our mom if we can come back and fish," Ronny replied.

Rita gave the boys twenty-five dollars and they fished that afternoon.

"It's fun to catch so many fish and to watch them take the bait," Ronny said when they brought the fish to Aunt Janie.

"Yes it is," Aunt Janie said. "It is a lot different than wading out into the streams and trying to catch them after they are dumped into the rivers." Janie cleaned the fish and put most of them in the freezer. "She fried the rest of them for supper.

"We don't eat fish very often since we live in cattle country," Rita said, "but, these are really good."

It was soon Sunday afternoon and time to start home. Rita, Danny, and Ronny packed their suitcases and put them into the Brown's car. Kimberly and Kristi took the doll clothes off Rascal and kissed him good-bye. Rascal kissed everyone on the cheek. Rita and the boys crawled into the car and waved good-bye.

"Come back and see us and bring Rascal with you," Aunt Janie said.

"Yes, he was very entertaining," said Uncle Bill.

"He is the best doll we ever had," Kimberly said.

"I love him!" little Kristi exclaimed.

"We will try to bring him back someday," Rita promised. She drove the car around the circle drive way and headed down the mountain toward the valley below.

"I want a pet like that, daddy," Kimberly said.

"Kimberly, raccoons are hard to find. They are hard to catch and they are usually too wild to tame. They can be very dangerous, and besides the government has made it against the law to capture them," Uncle Bill tried to explain.

"But daddy, Rascal isn't dangerous," Kimberly said.

"That's because Danny found him when he was just born. He doesn't even know he is a raccoon. He thinks he is a people person," Her father tried to explain.

Rascal crawled up in Danny's lap and was soon asleep.

"Mom, I forgot to fill Rascal's bottles before we left!" Danny exclaimed. "What are we going to do?" he asked.

"Your were having such a good time that I filled them for you," Rita replied.

"Cool. Thanks mom," Danny said.

Rascal drank all the milk from his bottle. He was so tired that he slept almost all the way home.

•   •   •

Chapter V

Visiting the Neighbors

Rascal spent the next week locked up in the laundry room alone while Rita and the boys were in school. Rita and Danny took turns coming home at noon and feeding him. Rascal's purring became louder and louder as he nursed his bottle.

Rascal was old enough for Danny to take to school just before summer vacation. He felt cool to have an unusual pet. The students carried Rascal around while he took barrettes out of the girl's hair and searched the boy's pockets for something sweet to eat.

"He acts like a spoiled child," one girl said.

"Yes he is a little spoiled," Danny agreed.

"He's the cutest, and funniest, pet I ever saw," one of Danny's friends said.

Maybe you can bring him back to school next fall and we can see how much he has grown," one teacher suggested.

"I would like to do that," Danny replied.

It had been a busy afternoon. Danny was tired by the time he put Rascal around his neck and crawled into the Brown's car to go home.

"How was your day?" Rita asked when she crawled into the car.

"Cool. Rascal was very entertaining," Danny replied. "Everyone would like to have a pet like him, but I'm the only person with a pet like this," he said giving Rascal a hug.

"And I'm reminded of it every day," Rita said, laughing.

School was soon out for the summer. Ronny and Danny were both working for their father at his farm implement business. Ronny was driving a truck and helping to set up large irrigation pumps to water the fields of corn and wheat. Danny worked in the shop where his grandfather repaired the engines. Rita was never lonesome with Rascal around. He did something different every day.

Rascal played with the dogs, Velvet and Mickey, while Rita mowed the grass, washed the car, and planted flowers. When Rita worked in the house Rascal would try to figure out what she was doing. Sometimes Rita would forget about Rascal until he ran up her body and jumped on top of the cabinet. "You are a lot of trouble but you are cute," Rita often said.

It was Memorial Day, the last weekend in May. This was the day families visited the graves of their family members that had died. Most of Rita's relatives had moved away but many of them returned every year to put flowers on the graves of family members.

Rita went with her mother and sister to decorate the graves of Rita's dad's parents and her mother's parents which were Rita's grandparents. They went a day early so the graves looked pretty when other people came into the cemeteries to decorate.

The next day Danny and Ronny were at work. Rita was doing the breakfast dishes when she saw a car pull into the driveway. She went to the door and recognized Aunt Marie and Aunt Edith, two of her father's sisters.

"Come in. It's good to see you," Rita yelled. She gave each aunt a hug as they came through the front door.

"It's good to see you too, Rita," Aunt Edith said. "Can you show me where your bathroom is located?" she asked.

"Sure," Rita answered. She led Aunt Edith down the hall and showed her the large hall bathroom. Aunt Edith went in and locked the door.

Aunt Edith sat down on the toilet. Rascal was asleep in the trash can. The noise woke him up. He opened his eyes and saw a bare leg. Rascal was curious, so he reach up and felt of the leg.

Aunt Edith saw the wild animal and thought she was being attacked. She screamed and ran from the bathroom. "There's a wild animal in there!" Aunt Edith screamed.

Rita laughed. "I guess he is a wild animal, but he doesn't know it." Rita said.

"I think he bit my leg"!" Aunt Edith screamed.

"Let me see," Rita said. She looked at Aunt Edith's leg. "There are no marks on your leg, Aunt Edith," she said.

"I guess it just scared me," Aunt Edith said. "What is it?" she asked.

"It's a baby raccoon," Rita answered. "Would you like to meet him?" she asked.

"I would like to see him," Aunt Marie said.

"I don't know if I would like to see him again or not!" Aunt Edith exclaimed.

"He won't hurt you, Aunt Edith," Rita said. "Come with me and I'll introduce you both to our unusual pet."

Aunt Marie followed Rita into the bedroom. Aunt Edith followed Aunt Marie. "I don't know if I want to see him again or not," Aunt Edith said again.

"Oh, come on, he won't hurt you," said Rita. She walked down the hall calling, "Here Rascal. Here Rascal. It's all right."

Rascal did not come out of his hiding place.

Rita searched the bedroom and looked on top al all the furniture. She finally got on her hands and knees and looked under the bed. "It's all right, Rascal," Rita said again. She petted the fury animal and gently pulled him out from under the bed. "I want you to meet my aunts," she said. "Aunt Marie and Aunt Edith I want to meet our pet raccoon, Rascal."

"Oh, isn't he cute," Aunt Marie said. She petted Rascal. "Can I hold him?" she asked.

"Maybe we better wait until he isn't frightened any longer," Rita said.

"I guess he is cute," Aunt Edith said. Her hand was still shaking as she started to pet Rascal.

Rascal crawled upon Rita's shoulders and hid behind her head. He peaked out from behind Rita's head at the two aunts.

"You really scared him," Rita said.

"He really scared me," said Aunt Edith.

Rascal was clinging to Rita's neck. "Come on into the kitchen and I'll fix you each a cup of coffee," she said. She led the aunts down the hall and to the kitchen.

"Are you going to fix our coffee with that raccoon still wrapped around your neck?" Aunt Marie asked. Both aunts started laughing.

"It seems like I'm learning to do a lot of things with Rascal wrapped around my neck, like cooking and driving. He does run and hide when I start the vacuum cleaner though," Rita replied.

Rita poured three cups of coffee and placed some home-made cookies on three small plates for her and her visitors. The women sit down at the dining room table to visit. Rascal was still wrapped around Rita's neck.

It was soon time for the aunts to leave.

"Thanks for stopping by," Rita said. "I always enjoy your visits. Stop by the next time you are in this area," she said as she walked her aunts to their car.

"Are you going to wear that fur scarf all day?" Aunt Marie asked.

"He used to lay on my neck a lot, but he is getting so much larger now that he makes my neck tried," Rita answered. She waved at the two aunts as they were driving away.

When Rascal felt safe, he jumped down and ran into the living room.

Rita washed off the coffee cups and plates and put them into the dish washer. She could still hear water running. Rita ran to the bathroom. "Oh no Rascal, don't swim in the stool!" Rita exclaimed. "I guess in all the excitement we left the lid up," she said.

Rita looked in the stool. Rascal looked like he was in a swimming pool. "Oh yuk! Now I'll have to take time to give you another bath!" she said. Rita put Rascal in the sink and scrubbed him with shampoo. "I'll be glad when you are too large to swim in the toilet," she said.

Rita had been planting flowers all morning. Rascal was tired from wrestling with Velvet and Mickey. They walked into the house together. Rita went to the bathroom and washed her hands. She dried her hands and went to the kitchen to fix a sandwich. Suddenly she heard strange noises. Rita ran back to the bathroom "I'm sure I put the lid down on the stool," she said.

"More cleaning," Rita sighed. The she started laughing. Rascal was sitting on the corner of the sink. He had the water turned on and was washing his tiny hands with soap. She

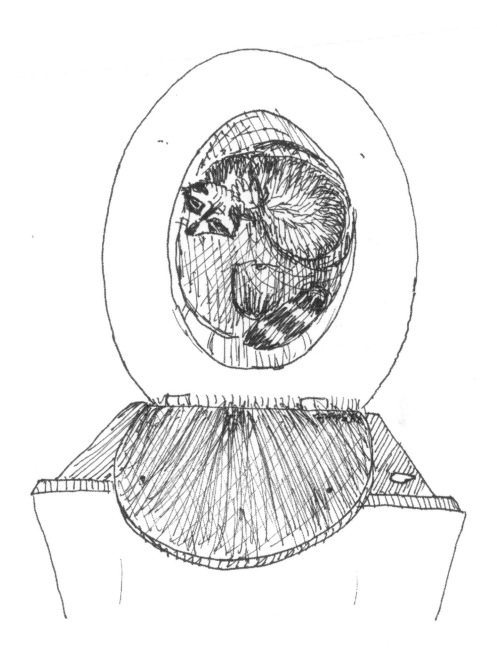

watched Rascal pull a washcloth from the towel bar and try to dry his hands. He still had soap all over his hands. "Rascal, what are you doing?" Rita shouted.

Rascal looked at Rita and jumped off the sink counter and ran from the room before Rita could catch him.

"Don't get soap on the carpet," Rita said. She grabbed a damp towel and tried to follow Rascal to clean up the soapy tracks. "I didn't know that coons were so fast," she said to herself. "Rascal, you are supposed to wash the soap off of your hands before you dry them. You are supposed to hang the towel up when you are finished, if you want to be a people person," she said.

Rascal looked at Rita and turned his head from side to side, and it sounded like he almost giggled.

Rita had to hurry to finish her work before her family came home for supper. "I'll be glad when Danny is here to take care of you and give me a break," she said.

The Browns discovered that coons are very curious. Ronny liked to put and empty box on the floor. Every time Rascal walked by, he would have to feel in every corner of the box until he was sure that there was nothing in it. Sometimes he would check a box a dozen times before he ignored it.

Rascal would turn boxes up-side-down and feel of everything that fell out. He emptied Rita's jewelry boxes, Danny and Ronny's school boxes, and Ray Brown's tool boxes.

"Danny, I think Rascal might be old enough to eat something besides nursing his bottle," Rita said. "He is growing so fast that he probably needs something more than milk."

"I don't know what to give him," Danny replied.

"Why don't you try feeding him some crumbled up bread in a pan of milk," Rita said. "It might be something like he is used to eating and he might like it."

Danny took a pie tin from the cabinet and put two slices of bread from the refrigerator. He crumbled the bread in the pan before he poured milk in it. Danny set the pan on the kitchen floor and went to find Rascal. He put Rascal on the floor in front of the pie tin.

Rascal sniffed at the bread and milk. He took his tiny hands and picked up some of the soaked bread. He pushed the bread into his mouth. Rascal ate all the bread and milk. He ate like he had been starving. Rascal had out grown his bottle and was now on a diet of bread and milk.

A few days later Rita caught Rascal eating cookies from the cookie jar. "Don't tell me that you have a sweet tooth," Rita said. "I'm going to have to put all the sweet things on the top shelves of the cabinets so you can't get into them," she told Danny's pet.

On Saturday morning Ray Brown was sitting in the living room reading the newspaper. He heard Rita running Rascal out of the kitchen. "Danny, I think Rascal is old enough to eat something besides bread and milk and the sweets he steals from your mother's kitchen," Ray said. "I think you should try feeding him some meat, and maybe he won't be hungry so often."

"How can I feed him meat?" Danny asked.

"You might try feeding him some canned dog food," his father answered.

Danny went into the kitchen and opened a can of meaty dog food. He put some of it in Rascal's pie tin. "Here Rascal. Here Rascal," Danny called. He rattled the pie tin the way he always did when he was calling Rascal to eat.

Rascal came running into the kitchen. Danny put the pie tin down in front of Rascal. Rascal sniffed at the meat and then he felt of it. It wasn't anything he wanted to eat so he walked away.

"Dad, he won't eat it," Danny called to his father.

"You can give that to the dogs, but try to get him to eat some dog food tomorrow," Ray Brown said. "He might have to see and smell it several times before he wants any."

Danny divided the fresh dog food between Velvet and Mickey. The dogs lapped it up quickly. They were used to dry dog food and thought the meaty dog food was a special treat.

The next day Danny gave Rascal some more dog food. Rascal walked away from it again. He tried and tried, but Rascal never wanted anything to eat except bread, milk, pies, cakes, and other sweets. He was a spoiled brat.

It was Thursday and the milk truck pulled into the driveway of the Brown home. It was his day to deliver milk, ice cream, and other diary products. "What do you need today?" the milkman asked.

"I need two gallons of milk. I also need to half gallons of ice cream. Make one chocolate and one vanilla," Rita answered.

"Yes mam," the milkman said. He brought in the products and put them into the refrigerator and freezer for Rita. "See you next week," he said.

Ten minutes later Rita saw the milk truck pull back up on their driveway. "Did you forget something?" she asked from the front door.

"No!" the man shouted.

Rita saw that the milkman was angry about something.

"I left here and went over to your neighbor's house to deliver their milk," the milkman said rather loudly. "When I opened the back door to get my products, there was a wild animal in there. He showed his teeth and growled at me. He won't let me in my truck and I can't get him out!" The man yelled. "Your neighbor said that the wild animal belongs to you." "Will you please come and get him so I can deliver the rest of my products?" the man begged.

"I'm so sorry," Rita said. She followed the milkman to the back of the truck.

The milkman opened the door. Rascal was sitting on top of a stack of cartons filled with milk.

"He probably thought he was in coon heaven when he found this place," Rita said, laughing as she stepped into the truck.

"Be careful lady," the milkman said.

"You naughty boy!" Rita exclaimed, scolding Rascal. She took hold of the back of Rascal's neck and pulled him from the milk throne.

"I guess he wasn't so wild after all," the milkman said, petting Rascal. "I'll be careful next time and shut the truck door when I get out."

Rascal crawled around Rita's neck and they watched the milk truck back away from the house. "I'm sorry for all the trouble Rascal made for you, and all the time you lost this morning," she called to the milkman.

A few days later Rascal was playing in the yard with big Mickey and seven-pound Velvet. He suddenly smelled something good. The neighbor lady had just backed two apple pies. She had set one apple pie in the open window to make it cool faster.

Mrs. Smith heard the doorbell ringing. "Come in," she told her friends. She pointed to two large chairs in the living room and said, "Sit down so we can visit. I haven't seen you guys for a long time." "How are you?" she asked.

A few minutes later Mrs. Smith said, "I have just made some apple pies. Would you like to have a piece of pie with some ice cream?"

"That sounds great!" the man said and the woman shook her head to agree.

Mrs. Smith went into the kitchen to get her pie from the open window. Rascal was dipping his tiny hands into the pie and eating as fast as he could eat. Pie filling was all over his face. Mrs. Smith started laughing. "Come quick! I don't imagine you have ever seen anything like this before!" she called to her friends.

The friends ran into the kitchen.

"The little Rascal sure is cute," the lady said, She did not know that was his name.

"Where did he come from?" the man asked, laughing.

"He belongs to our neighbor's son," Mrs. Smith said.

There was not much pie left. Rascal took a few more quick bites and jumped down from the window sill. He ran back into his own yard before he started cleaning off his face.

Mrs. Smith fixed the second pie for her friends. That afternoon she called Rita. "Rita, I baked some apple pies this morning and I set one in an open window to cool." "Do you know what happened?" she asked.

"I think I can guess," Rita answered. "Rascal was outside this morning and he just loves sweets. I'm so sorry for any damage he might have done," she said.

"Don't feel bad," Mrs. Smith said while laughing, "It was worth losing the pie just to see the little feller in action. "I guess he needs his mask if he is going to be a pie bandit."

"I appreciate your attitude about it and not getting mad over it," Rita replied.

Rascal could not keep away from water. He was constantly trying to swim in the bathroom toilet, even when he was too big and he was always turning on faucets. The Browns were constantly turning off faucets in the bathrooms, the kitchen, and even in the yard.

Danny enjoyed sitting in the bath tub and watching Rascal swim around him. Rascal was much more graceful in water than when he was walking. The rest of the family had to always lock the bathroom door when they took a bath or they would have a wild animal in the tub with them while they were trying to bathe. If the door was not locked, Rascal could open it with his long claws, take one long jump, and land right in the tub. The masked bandit would swim around any person that was in the tub whether they wanted him there or not.

While in the water, Rascal's tail worked like a rudder of a ship. It turned him around quickly any direction he wanted to go.

Rita had just come in from working in the yard. Ronny and a couple of his high school friends were watching TV in the family room. Rita went to the bathroom and turned on the bath water and put in some bubble bath. She went to the bedroom and gathered up some clean clothes. Rita returned to the bathroom and thought she had locked the door. She stepped into the warm water and bubbles and began to relax. Rita heard Ronny and his friends talking as they walked past the bathroom door to his bedroom. They had just passed the bathroom door when the door flew open.

Rascal ran into the bathroom and did not close the door. He made one dive and landed in the tub right next to Rita. He was scooting around her just like a motor boat.

Rita jumped out of the tub and ran for the door before the boys had a chance to come back down the hall. "I didn't know I could move that fast!" Rita exclaimed.

Rascal jumped out of the tub and ran for the door. This time the door was locked and he could not get out. There was bubble bath everywhere. Rita had to towel—dry off herself, Rascal, and the whole bathroom. "At least you are clean again," she told the wild animal.

Rita was cleaning house Saturday morning. She had just turned off the vacuum cleaner when the telephone rang. It was another neighbor.

"Rita, this coon of Danny's . . . ." the neighbor said.

"Oh no! What is Rascal into now?" Rita exclaimed.

"He is in our house. He is in our bread drawer, and we can't get him out," the neighbor said.

"I'm terribly sorry. I'll be right over," Rita said.

Danny was five blocks away practicing baseball at the baseball field. Rita did not have time to go after him. She ran over to her neighbor's house as fast as she could run. Mrs. Binder held the door open for Rita.

Rita ran into the kitchen. There was Rascal sitting in one of the cabinet drawers. He was eating a cinnamon roll.

"He just loves sweets," Rita said. She grabbed Rascal by the back of the neck and pulled him from the bread drawer. "You are lucky he didn't go swimming in your bathroom stool," she said.

"He did that before he crawled into the bread drawer," Mr. Binder said. He was laughing. "Don't blame Rascal. I let him in. I thought when he had gotten into enough things I'd pick him up and put him back outside. I found out that if I tried to pick him up, he would bite me. I thought I better have you come over and get him," he said.

"Danny, Ronny, and I are about the only people that can pick him up when he doesn't want bothered," Rita explained. "Shame on you," she told Rascal. She hugged the furry animal and took Danny's unusual pet back home.

Rita was telling the Brown family about Rascal's visit to the Bender's. "Will you look at that," Ray Brown said, pointing to the living room.

Everyone turned around to see what was going on. Velvet and Rascal were wrestling in the middle of the floor. Velvet had started to growl. "Rascal is wrestling with Velvet and he has a hammerlock hold on her. He looks almost human," Ronny said.

Rascal grabbed Velvet's leg again and started to turn it the wrong way. He put pressure on it until it started to hurt. Velvet growled and Rascal let her up. The two animals stood up facing each other again. Rascal grabbed Velvet's hind foot again and pinned her down. Velvet growled again and Rascal let her up.

"That's funny," Danny said. "Rascal could kill Velvet in a few seconds, if he wanted to. He has such sharp claws and teeth. But, Velvet thinks she is the boss and Rascal has decided not to hurt her."

The rest of the family agreed.

Chapter VI

Summer Camp

"Danny, would you like to go to church camp this year?" Rita asked. "I'm going as a counselor, and I would be happy if you would go with me. It is your age group that is going next week," she said.

"I don't know if dad will let me off work," Danny replied. "It would be fun to be gone for a week, and we can take Rascal with us."

"I'll give you a week off work, but I think that taking Rascal would be too much for the camp to put up with," Ray Brown said, laughing.

"What can we do with Rascal while we are gone?" Danny asked.

"I can take care of him," Ronny said.

"I don't think that is a good idea," Rita replied. "You will be gone too many hours during the day. We might not have a house left when you get home from work," she explained.

"Then, what can we do with him?" Danny asked. "I know. Maybe grandma would take care of him for us," he said, answering his own question.

"He is so much trouble, I don't have the nerve to ask anyone else," Rita said. "Why don't you telephone your grandma right now and ask her?"

"I'm glad you're going to church camp, and of course we'll take care of Rascal for you," grandma said. "I think Rascal will be happy with us for a few days."

"Thanks grandma. I hope he doesn't cause you too much trouble," Danny said. "We will be leaving early next Monday morning so we will bring him to your house on Sunday."

"We'll see you then," grandma said and hung up.

Rita and Danny took Rascal to Rita's mother' Sunday afternoon. Rascal was too busy running up and down the fruit trees to tell Danny and Rita good-bye.

"I hope he won't be too much trouble for you, mother," Rita said again.

"Don't worry dear. He'll be just fine," grandma said. "You just go on and have a good time, and don't worry about Rascal."

"I know Rascal will be all right," Rita said, laughing, "I just hope that you and Daddy will be all right after a week with Rascal."

The next morning Rita and Danny boarded the old church bus with two other sponsors and twenty, fifth, sixth, and seventh graders. The older people visited while the kids played games, talked, listened to their tapes and slept.

The camp was located along the Arkansas River in another state. It would take six hours to get there.

Several hours later, half way across Kansas, the clouds turned dark. The thunder was so loud that no one could talk and be heard. The wind was changing directions every few minutes. When the clouds lifted, everyone yelled, "Look!" There were at least three tornadoes dropping from the sky around them.

Betty, one of the sixth grade girls, ran to Rita and hid her face in Rita's chest. She had been one of Rita's students and she felt safer in Rita's arms. "Mrs. Brown, we are going to hit by tomatoes!" she screamed.

Everyone had to laugh even though they were all frightened.

The old bus swayed with the strong winds. The children were sitting up straight with their hands clinging to the back of the seat in front of them. There were damaged towns, fields, and telephone lines on each side of the road. One town's airport had been entirely destroyed by a tornado. The storm was still swirling around. The kids were still and wondering if they were going to make it to their destination or not.

They were too far from home to turn back. There was no place that looked safe to turn off the highway. The bus driver, that was also the pastor, drove carefully through the rubble and on toward the church camp. It was even scarier after dark.

Finally the old bus turned off the highway toward the camp located in the back of many trees. "Praise the Lord we make it!" the pastor yelled when he could see the cabins at the camp. Preacher Joe was so happy that he started honking the bus horn.

"Let's drive around the circle road through the camp and honk the horn to celebrate," one of the kids said.

"Yeah!" everyone agreed. They were all thanking God for their safety as Preacher Joe drove around the road shaped like a heart. He was honking the horn.

"Everyone must be glad to see us?" Rita exclaimed. "They are all running into the large dining room building and screaming."

Preacher Joe parked the bus in front of the dining hall. People were still running into the dining hall and screaming.

"Did we cause all this excitement?" Preacher Joe asked another sponsor?"

"Yes and no," the camp director said. "There has been a tornado warning here all day. We kept all the kids in the cabins for safety. If a tornado was spotted coming out way, our signal was to drive around the heart and honk our horns so everyone could run into this building for safety. When we heard your bus horn, we thought a tornado was right on us."

"Oh no,!" Preacher Joe exclaimed, "We are sorry to have scared everyone. We were just celebrating our own safety."

"Attention everyone," the director said over his megaphone, "This has been a false alarm. Everyone can come on out from under the tables."

Workers and kids started coming out from under the tables and from closets. Everyone was relieved and started laughing. It was too late for an evening meeting, but a great supper was served to two-hundred hungry kids and fifty workers. It was then time for everyone to go to their cabins and get ready for bed.

Rita was assigned eight girls in a half of cabin space to be her responsibility. Nancy, the other counselor was taking care of the other half of the cabin and her eight girls. She was friendly and Rita hoped that Danny was having as much fun as she was.

Rita relaxed and sat on a large rock the next morning to listen to a Bible class. It was interesting. Suddenly her waist started to itch under the wide belt she was wearing. Rita became so miserable that she went to the camp nurse to see what was wrong.

The nurse pulled up Rita's shirt and examined her. She took several minutes before she said, "You have thirty-two chiggers."

"What are chiggers?" Rita asked.

"I can't believe that you don't know!" the nurse exclaimed. "They are tiny insects that dig into your skin and hair pores and stay there and eat until they die," the nurse explained. "They can make you miserable, but they are not dangerous. The only thing you can do is try to kill them so they will come out of your skin."

"Yuck!" Pam replied. "How do you kill them?" she asked.

"Kerosene is just as good as medicine. I'll dab each of them now with it and you can put more kerosene on them whenever they start itching," the nurse answered.

"That does feel better," Rita said as the nurse put kerosene on each of her thirty-two welts. "It's terrible to think I'm carrying around that many insects in my skin. I feel like a flea circus."

"I advise you not to wear belts or any clothing that makes you sweat and don't sit on the grass or rocks. It has been damp this year and the chiggers are really bad," the nurse explained.

"It is dry where I live so I have never seen chiggers until now," said Rita.

The counselors called the kids to get up at 6:30 every morning. The boys stayed in the cabins east of the large chapel and dining room, and the girls stayed on the west side. Each area had an extra building where the commodes, ten shower stalls, and ten sinks were located.

Nancy and Rita watched as the girls washed their faces, put on makeup, and curled their hair. Some of the girls primped in front of the two large mirrors hanging on the walls of the sleeping cabins. One of the girls used such a strong hair spray that she ran from the cabin after spraying her hair. Everyone else had to run from the cabin before they started coughing too.

A large breakfast was served each morning between seven and eight o'clock. The counselors and kids met in the in the chapel after breakfast for a short Bible reading and prayer time before the kids were separated into small groups for art projects. Some of the kids made things out of wood and painted them to take home. Others drew or painted pictures. Some kids made things like cups and saucers on the potter's wheel. They put them in a kiln and baked them after painting them.

Lunch was served from 11:30 to 12:30. After dinner the kids attended Bible classes, and then were dismissed to go to the dining hall where they could buy candy, pop, gum, and pastries. After recess the students could to choose to go swimming in the new pool, or play volleyball, baseball, or go with a guide on a long hike. Danny had a hard time choosing between swimming and baseball and tried to do some of each.

Dinner was served between six and seven in the evening. The kids rushed back to the cabins to get cleaned up for the evening church service. There was more fun and games after the service.

One night the evening service was called a Beach Party. The students sat on sleeping mats instead of chairs and wore bright-colored clothes and hats.

Two services were held around camp fires. Everyone sang songs and roasted wieners to make hot dogs and roasted marsh mellows for smores.

On Tuesday night Rita was tired and crawled into bed as soon as her girls were in bed. The lights were off when her skin started itching again. This time she realized that the sheets felt ruff and sticky. Rita crawled out of bed and turned on cabin light. She pulled back the covers. Sweetened cereal had been dumped into her bed. "I hope Danny and his friends are not doing things like this to their counselors," Rita said to herself.

Rita heard giggling as she was cleaning out her bed. "Thanks a lot," she said. Rita took the sheets off her bed and took them outside to shake them. "I guess the squirrels and birds can have this for breakfast," she said. It didn't take Rita long go to sleep the second time she crawled into bed.

After chapel service Thursday night, the counselors hid in different places all around the camp. The kids had to find their counselors before they could go back to the dining room for more fun.

Rita hid in some tall weeds close to the baseball diamond. She watched through the weeds as her girls looked everywhere for her. She saw other groups take their counselors to the dining room for fun. Rita's girls could not find her. They finally gave up and Rita came out of the weeds. She received a prize but her girls were not happy that she had hidden so well. It had taken up too much of their fun time to look for her.

Rita made a special time to talk with each of her girls when they were alone. One of the girls was very sad and angry. Her older sister had died in a car accident the month before camp.

Suzy was mad at God and everyone else because of her sister's death. Rita listened as Suzy talked about her sister and the fun times they had had together.

"Suzy, I know it is hard to give up your sister, but to be mad at God and everyone else is not good for you," Rita tried to explain. "I don't know why your sister had to die, but I know that your anger will cause you to be sick."

Suzy fell into Rita's arms and cried. She prayed with Rita to forgive everyone, even God, and to go on with her life. Suzy was smiling for the first time since the accident. She left the cabin jumping up and down like she was free again.

One night Rita was helping her girls gather sticks for the large bond fire. There would be singing and a chapel service around the fire. Everyone was getting ready to roast wieners for hot dogs again.

Rita saw one girl reach over and pick up a stick. She noticed the ground where the girl had picked up the stick had a pretty design. Pam ran over to the girl and pulled her away from the spot. The girl had picked up the stick off of a copperhead snake. "Thank God it didn't bite you!" Rita exclaimed. "They are very poisonous.

The rest of the girls came running to see the snake. It looked like some kind of beautiful tapestry. One of the men heard the screams and came running. He took a hoe and killed the snake. The snake was put into a large jar for all the people to see. The kids were careful the rest of the week, but no one else saw any more snakes.

"The snakes probably go running when they hear all the people noises at camp time," one counselor said laughing.

Rita went swimming with her eight girls one afternoon at the new pool. At the entrance of the pool was a small statue of a young man Rita had known. He had been the son of one of her ministers.

David had graduated from high school and started to college. He and two friends went swimming that fall in a large lake near their school. David dove into the lake and never came up. The sheriff said that he had gotten tangled up in the algae at the bottom of the lake and could not come up for air.

The churches dedicated the new pool to David's memory and named the pool after him.

"That statue sure looks like him," Rita told her girls.

It was soon Friday afternoon and time to go home. The kids had had so much fun during the week that they were not ready to go home. They were exchanging address and telephone numbers with their new friends. There were hugs and tears as everyone said good-bye. Preacher Joe headed the old bus west as the group started their six hour trip back home.

The kids were soon asleep as the bus swayed down the highway. Rita enjoyed talking with Preacher Joe and the other counselors.

Rita and Danny went after Rascal as soon as they came home. Danny was glad to see his little friend and Rita hugged Rascal too.

"What did Rascal get into while we were gone?" Rita asked.

Rita's mother laughed and said, "Everything! He kept your dad and me laughing the whole time you were gone."

"I hope he wasn't an awful lot of work for you, grandma," Danny said.

"He was a lot of work, but we enjoyed watching him," grandma said. "He is so different from other animals. One of the funniest things he did while you were gone was to wet on the bathroom floor."

"I don't think that's very funny," Danny replied.

"That wasn't but I scolded him for making a mess and went after a mop to clean it up," grandma explained. "When I came back with the mop, Rascal had one of my best towels. He was trying to clean up his own mess," grandma said with a chuckle.

"I'm glad you can laugh about it, grandma," Danny said.

"We also had a picnic while you were gone. Everyone was getting their drinks when they noticed that Rascal was picking up the food he wanted right off of everyone's plate," said grandma.

"You bad boy," Danny scolded shaking his finger at Rascal.

"He is one experience we will never forget," grandma said.

Danny carried Rascal to the car. He and Rita waved good-bye. "Thanks for taking care of him for us," Danny and Rita said again.

Chapter VII

A Trip to New Mexico

It was August and school would soon be starting.

"Danny, how would you like to go to New Mexico to see cousin Mandy and her family before school starts?" Rita asked.

"Cool. That sounds like fun and more fun if we can take Rascal," Danny answered.

Dick was a year older than Danny and Rusty was a year younger. They had a little sister, Patti Jo, who was only six years old.

Rita telephoned Mandy. "Are you going to be home next week and can we come to visit you?" Rita asked.

"Sure! I'm excited that you are coming to see us," Mandy answered.

"Mandy, Danny has a little pet raccoon. We wondered if you would mind if we brought Rascal along with us?" Rita asked.

"Ray and Ronny have to stay home and work so there will only be Danny, me, and Rascal," she explained.

"That sounds great. We have never been around a raccoon before. I think it will be fun to meet him," Cousin Mandy said.

Rascal was well behaved during the three hour trip. He played with Danny for awhile and then he curled up around Rita's neck and slept the rest of the way. Rascal was so relaxed that he did not make Rita's neck tired.

Mandy and her children saw the Brown's car drive up to the house and came out to greet them.

"So this is the little feller you were telling me about!" Mandy exclaimed when he saw Rascal around Rita's neck.

"Yes," Rita answered with a smile.

Everyone patted Rascal before Danny took him from his mother's neck. The kids took Rascal to the back of the house to play. Dick and Rusty were soon showing Danny their new motorcycles. The boys forgot about Rascal as they rode the motorcycles.

Bob was still at work. Mandy fixed Rita and herself a glass of ice tea. The women took the ice tea to the dining room to sit down and visit.

Mandy looked pretty. She had just come home from the Beauty Shop. Her hair was styled beautifully on the top of her head. About twenty-five bobby pins were hidden in her hair to keep it in place.

Rascal came back into the house. He crawled up Rita's chair and curled around her neck again.

"He sure is a cute little feller," Mandy said again. "May I hold him?" she asked.

"Sure," Rita answered. She pulled Rascal from her neck and laid him in Mandy's lap.

Mandy patted Rascal. Rascal lay in Mandy's lap a few minutes and then he crawled up on her shoulders. Rascal curled around Mandy's neck. The two women talked about the many things that had happened since their last visit.

"What are you doing?" Mandy asked when a section of her hair fell to her shoulders. She saw some bobby pins fall to the floor. "Oh, you're taking down my hair," Mandy said laughing.

"Rascal, don't do that!" Rita yelled. She started to pick up Rascal.

"It's all right. It isn't every day that a person gets to have a raccoon around their neck, even if he is messing up my hair," Mandy said laughing.

Rascal loved hair pins. He soon had all of the pins pulled out of Mandy' hair. The curls fell to Mandy's shoulders in a tangled mess and the pins fell to the floor.

Mandy just laughed and said, "You little rascal."

Rita helped Mandy fry some chicken and fix a salad for supper. Rita had a hard time keeping Rascal out of the salad. She saw the boys ride in on their motorcycles and called for Danny to come get this "pesky animal" until supper time.

Danny was not through riding the cycles with Dick and Rusty. "Rascal likes to play dolls," Danny told Patti Jo. "Do you have a doll buggy?" he asked.

"Yes!" Patti Jo exclaimed. She ran into her bedroom and came out with a new doll buggy. "I got this last Christmas," Patti Jo said.

Danny put Rascal into the doll buggy. Patty Jo pushed him around the house until supper was ready. This gave Danny and her brothers more time to ride through town on their motorcycles.

Bob came home from work. He stopped at the door to stare at the wild animal standing in the middle of the door.

"Grrr," said Rascal.

"Shame on you, Rascal," Rita said, picking up the raccoon.

"Isn't he a cure little feller," Mandy asked, petting Rascal.

"He sure is. I guess he was just trying to act wild when I tried to come through the door," Bob replied. Since Bob was taller than Mandy and Rita, Rascal was soon wrapped around Bob's neck looking down on every one else. He was put in one of the bedrooms and the door was shut so everyone could eat supper without being disturbed.

"I feel bad about locking him in the bedroom," Mandy said.

"I don't want him trying to eat out of everyone's plate," Danny explained. "This is good food, Mandy." He said as he started to eat.

"Thank you," Mandy replied.

When everyone finished eating, Danny opened the bedroom door to let Rascal out. He had to go in and pick up clothes from off the floor that Rascal had pulled off the bed.

Rita helped Mandy to clean up the kitchen while the boys played a new game in Dick's room. Patty Jo dressed Rascal in some doll clothes. Bob thought Rascal was very interesting and laughed when he saw him in the doll clothes.

"I think I will pop some popcorn for us to eat while we are watching TV," Mandy said. She put the popcorn popper on the stove and popped enough popcorn to fill her largest bowl. Mandy took the popcorn into the living room and called the kids to come and eat.

Just as Mandy handed the large bowl to Bob, Rascal jumped for the bowl. The bowl went up in the air and popcorn flew in every direction like an explosion. Rascal jumped to the floor and started to eat the popcorn as fast as he could eat.

"Cool!" the kids shouted.

"You little rascal," Mandy said. She and Rita got down on their hands and knees and picked up the popcorn from the furniture and floor, and even in the dining room floor and furniture.

After the mess was cleaned up, Mandy popped more corn. "Keep a good hold on that bowl when you pass it," she told everyone. There were several pieces of popcorn accidentally dropped on the floor for Rascal.

"It is time for your baths." Mandy told the kids.

"Would you like for Rascal to bathe with us?" Danny asked.

"Sounds like fun," both Rusty and Dick replied.

The boys went to the bathroom and started filling the tub with water. When they opened the bathroom door, Rascal ran into the bathroom. He made one long jump and landed in the bath water. The boys took turns climbing into the tub with Rascal. Rascal enjoyed swimming around them just like a ship.

"He looks like a motor boat," Rusty said.

"Yes, because he uses his tail like a rudder," Dick agreed.

Patti Jo took her turn bathing with Rascal after the boys were finished. Rita helped Mandy clean up a very wet bathroom.

About that time Dick's basset hound dog came into the house for the night. He lay down in his favorite spot on a rug by the kitchen door. Rascal ran up to the dog and made one of his horrible noises. The dog howled in fear and ran out of the house. He went over to the neighbor's house and stayed until the company was gone.

Rascal slept between Dick and Danny in Dick's room. "I need to warn you that Rascal might bite your toes on pinch you nose while you are asleep." Danny said, "If you keep your sheet pulled tightly over your head, you should be all right."

Rascal woke the boys up several times during the night. Rita could hear the boys laughing. "I wonder what Rascal is doing now?" she asked herself.

The next morning Mandy cooked bacon and eggs for breakfast. Rita cooked pancakes. "I can't believe how much growing boys eat," Rita said.

"Don't I know it!" Mandy exclaimed.

After breakfast the boys went riding on the motor cycles again. "Be careful and only ride on the back streets," Mandy yelled through the screen door."

Patti Jo took Rascal to her room and put doll clothes on him again.

Rita helped Mandy clean up the kitchen again. They sit down at the kitchen table to do more visiting. "Oh you little rascal!" Mandy exclaimed.

Rita turned around to see what Rascal was doing now. "Oh no!" she screamed. Rascal was dragging everything out from under the beds. There were several pieces of women's personal clothing that no one else should see. "Rascal, don't do that!" Rita yelled.

Rascal dropped the clothing he was carrying and ran out of the bedroom.

Rita helped Mandy pick up all the things Rascal had drug out from under the beds and from some drawers. The women made the beds and straightened up the house while Patti Jo kept Rascal busy by pushing him in the doll buggy. Mandy was fixing some lunch when the boys came back from their motor cycle rides.

"They have a cool obstacle trail out south of town, Mom," Danny said. "Would you like for me to show it to you?" he asked.

"If you think I can hold on that well," Rita answered. She crawled on the cycle behind Danny and put her arms tightly around his waist. Rusty jumped on behind Dick and they followed Danny and Rita out of town.

Rita enjoyed the breeze blowing through her hair and looking at the small town where her relatives lived.

They were soon out of town and speeding down a dirt path. Danny drove up and down hills, over large bumps, and through a mud puddle. Rita was hanging on tight, but enjoying the ride. Danny drove around for about thirty minutes.

"We need to get back to the house for lunch," Rita yelled over the noise of the cycle. They headed back to town.

Rita helped Mandy finish lunch and the boys went to Dick's room to look at Dick's stamp collection.

"Mom, come here quick!" Dick yelled. "Rascal is fishing in my fish aquarium!"

The mothers ran to Dick's bedroom. Rascal was sitting on the edge of the large aquarium. He was dipping his hands into the water. He was so fast that he caught one of the larger tropical fish.

"Grab him Danny before he gets away!" Rita yelled.

Danny grabbed Rascal and Pam grabbed Rascal's hand. She shook it until the fish dropped back into the water.

Rascal jumped down from the aquarium and ran from the room.

"Thanks Aunt Rita," Dick said. "That was one of my favorite fish. It came from Africa and I don't know if I could ever find another one or not."

"You need to keep your bedroom door shut and locked the rest of the time we are here," Rita said. "Fishing is something that is natural to raccoons and I'm sure he will try it again if he has a chance.

The boys rode the cycles all afternoon while Patti Jo played dolls with Rascal. The kids took turn bathing with Rascal again Saturday night.

Rita locked Rascal in the bathroom before everyone went to church Sunday morning. All the towels, washcloths, toothpaste, and combs were in the middle of the floor when they came home, but the rest of the house and the fish had been safe. Rita cleaned up the bathroom while Bob helped Mandy fix lunch.

It was another good meal. Rita was helping Mandy clean up the kitchen when Danny yelled through the back door, "Mom, we're going to ride the motor cycles again."

"It is time for us to start home now," Rita answered. "You will have to wait until we come back next time, if Mandy and her family will let us come back next time after all the trouble Rascal has caused."

"Oh it's been the most fun we have had for a long time," Mandy replied with a smile. "He's one experience we will never forget."

Danny and Rita packed their suitcases and put them into the car. "Where is Rascal?" Rita asked.

Danny went to the back door and called for Rascal. He heard a strange noise that sounded like a wolf. Danny went outside and looked up. Rascal was climbing to the top of the tallest tree on the street.

Danny climbed up the tree toward Rascal. Every time he was almost close enough to grab Rascal, Rascal jumped to another branch further away. Rascal was having a lot of fun. Danny was trying to keep from falling.

Danny heard people laughing beneath him. He looked down and it looked like the whole town had gathered under the tree to watch him and Rascal. Danny felt embarrassed. "Come here Rascal!" he yelled.

Rascal chattered like a bird and jumped the other way.

"Rascal, stay there so I can pick you up. We have to go home," Danny said softly.

It took four more branches and a lot of soft talking before Rascal let Danny grab him. The crowd at the bottom of the tree was cheering. Danny felt his face turning red from embarrassment as he tried to keep hold of Rascal and climb back down the tall tree. Rascal helped a little by holding on to Danny's neck.

It seemed to take a long time for Danny to get half way down the tree. Rusty climbed the tree and helped Danny the rest of the way. Rusty took Rascal and let Danny climb down onto a lower branch.

Danny took Rascal while rusty climbed down to a lower branch just like Alan and Danny did climbing down from the tall trees at Alan's grandpa's creek.

"Thanks, Rusty" Danny said when they were both safely on the ground.

The crowd was still waiting to get a better view of the "wild animal".

"Cool," several kids said as they petted Rascal.

The crowd made some comments about Rascal that Danny had heard many times. Danny held his pet tightly and crawled into the Brown's car.

Rita hugged each of her relatives good-bye and Rascal kissed Mandy and her family good-bye.

"Thanks for bringing the little rascal along so we could meet him," Mandy said.

"Thanks for not getting mad when he was a bad boy," Rita said.

"He is one experience we will never forget," said Bob.

"Neither will your neighbors," Danny replied with a tired sigh.

Everyone waved good-by. Rita turned the car north and they started their two-hour trip home. Danny was soon asleep in the back seat and Rascal was soon asleep around Rita's neck again.

Chatper VIII

All about Animals

Rita and Danny did not get home in time to go to church that Sunday evening. The next Sunday evening Rita changed into her good clothes and ready to go church when she noticed it was not quite time to leave. "I think I will go into the family room and watch TV with the rest of the family until it is time for me leave," Rita said to herself.

Ray Brown was relaxing in his favorite cushioned chair. Ronny was sitting in the large chair Rita usually sat in. Danny was lying on a part of the sectional couch. Rita decided to sit on one of the cushioned footstools since she didn't have much time.

Rascal had been asleep on Danny's feet on the couch. He woke up when Rita came into the room. Rascal crawled up into Pam's lap and went back to sleep. He was so large that his head dropped off on one side of Rita's lap, and his back legs dropped off the other side of her lap. His long, soft, ringed tail lay on the carpet.

Rascal felt heavy in Rita's lap. Rita moved to keep from getting a cramp in her leg. At the same time Ronny looked at Rascal and made a terrifying loud noise.

The horrible noise scared Rascal so much that he wet all over Rita. She felt the hot liquid soaking through her clothes and running down her legs. "Oh yuck!" Rita exclaimed. "What did you do that for?" Rita asked Ronny.

By this time Ronny was laughing too hard to talk. Ray Brown and Danny were laughing too.

Rita jumped up from the footstool and ran for the bathroom.

Poor Rascal ran and hid behind the couch.

Rita had to take a bath and put on another set of clean clothes. She could still hear her family laughing in the family room when she left for church. This was one time Rita could not laugh at something Rascal had done. It was a long time before she could laugh about it. She was glad no one asked her why she was late that night. It would have been embarrassing to explain.

The summer weeks passed quickly. Ronny and Danny were still working with their father at the irrigation shop. Besides working, the boys had at least three baseball games a week. Rascal helped the dogs watch the Brown's yard and he loved to go to the baseball games. He always had a crowd of people around him that thought he was interesting. Many kids said they would like to have a pet like him.

One Sunday afternoon the Browns were watching TV when Ray Brown said, "The weather is nice today. Let's go for a ride in the country. There are some irrigation pumps I want to check south of town."

Rascal ran to the car with the rest of the family. He did not wait for an invitation. They were about ten miles out of town when Rita asked, "Where is Rascal?"

"I thought he was in the front seat with you and Dad," Danny said.

"He isn't up here anywhere," Rita replied. "He has to be in the back with you boys?"

"I don't see him anywhere!" everyone exclaimed.

"He has to be somewhere," Ray Brown said.

"He is too big to hide in the car," said Ronny.

Just then there was a growling noise from somewhere behind the dash of the car.

"Dad stop the Car!" Danny yelled. "Rascal is caught under the dash and I'm afraid he might grab an electrical wire and kill himself."

"If he got in there by himself, he can get out by himself!" Ray Brown exclaimed. He continued to drive on down the road.

The Browns heard a lot of banging and clanking behind the dash. They heard more growls.

"I'm afraid he will tear all the wires loose from the tape player and other things that are under the dash." Rita said.

Ray Brown stopped the car. The Browns watched to see what was going to happen to Rascal.

"I sure hope he doesn't hurt himself," said Danny.

There was a thud in the glove compartment of the car. Everyone was staring at the dash. "Rascal is too large to get into the glove compartment," everyone said.

Rita carefully opened the door of the glove compartment and out tumbled Rascal. It looked like there was no way that he could fit into that tiny space, but he did.

"He is just like a rat," Ronny remarked, "He can squeeze through a space half as big as he is."

Rascal curled up in Rita's lap and slept the rest of the trip. Nothing on the car seemed to be torn up. Rascal did not wake up to look out the car window when Ray Brown drove through several fields. The crops were about ready to harvest. The roads were bumpy, but Rascal still did not wake up and the car and seemed not to be damaged.

The guys were at work one day when the telephone rang. Rita answered.

"Someone told us that you have a pet raccoon at your house," a woman said. It was Edna, an older woman from the church.

"We most surely do!" Rita said, laughing.

"We have never seen one up close," Edna said. "Would you mind bringing him to our house so that my family and I can see him?" she asked.

"I don't mind. He loves to ride in the car," Rita answered.

Rascal climbed into the car with Rita. He sat on her shoulders so he could watch where they were going. Rita drove across town. "I probably have the furriest neck scarf in town," she said as Rascal curled around her neck again. "Edna is a very particular house keeper so please be good while we are there," Rita instructed. "Oh well, they did invite us over," She said to herself and Rascal.

Rascal was nice. He stayed in Rita's arms and did not try to get away or bite anyone.

"Isn't he cute?" Edna exclaimed. "Look at his tiny front feet. They almost look like a real baby's hands!" Edna felt of Rascal's feet. "They are as soft as a baby's hands too," she said.

Rascal looked at Edna and turned his head from one side to the other. He sat up in Rita's arms, grabbed one of Edna's hands and felt of her hand and fingers.

"You have a very special pet," Edna said while everyone was laughing.

"He usually puts on a good show," Rita said, "We need to go home now so I can finish supper for my family. It is almost time for Ray and the boys to be coming home from work."

"May I take a picture of Rascal before you leave?" Edna asked. "I would like to have a picture to remember how pretty he is," she said. "I'll have two pictures made and give you one."

"I think that's a great idea," Rita said. "The only others pictures we have of him is a movie my aunt took when he was nursing his bottle as a baby."

Rascal sat up straight in Rita's arms. He sat real still for his picture. His fluffy body filled Rita's arms. Rascal's long tail almost touched the floor. He smiled for his only picture.

"I'll order two pictures and bring yours to church when they come in," Edna said.

"Thank you for bringing Rascal over to meet us," Ted, Edna's husband, said.

The next morning Ray Brown left for work early. Ronny drove his car to work a little later. Danny rode his motorcycle to work a little later. Rita let Rascal outside to play with Velvet and Mickey. She was busy cleaning up the kitchen when she heard someone on the front porch. Rita looked through the kitchen window to see who was there.

Rita did not see anyone but Rascal. He was standing up on his hind feet and was reaching as far up as he could reach. Rascal was just tall enough to reach the storm door handle. He pulled the handle, pushed claws inside the door, and pulled the door open. Then he jumped up against the inside door. Rascal was just long enough to reach the front door knob. He grabbed the door knob and twisted it. Rascal used his claws again to pull the heavy door open.

Rascal ran into the house before the door closed. He ran to the refrigerator and used his claws to open the door to the freezer side. Rascal pulled himself up to the ice tray and fished around the ice bin until he found the piece of ice he wanted. He took the ice over to his water bowl and washed it several times. The small piece of ice melted. Rascal looked all around the dish for his piece of ice. He looked at Rita. He thought that Rita has stolen his piece of ice.

Rita laughed. "I guess you do wash everything you eat, but it won't work with ice," she said.

That evening the rest of the family watched Rascal open the two front doors, take ice out of the freezer and wash it. They all laughed when Rascal could not figure out what happened to the piece of ice.

The next morning the door bell rang. Rita opened the door and saw her friend, Irene. "Come in. I'm just about to rest with my second cup of coffee," Rita said. "Would you like to join me?" she asked.

"Sure, I guess I have a few minutes before I go on to town to shop," Irene replied. "And, what do you have here?" she asked when she saw Rascal coming to the table.

"This is Danny's pet raccoon," Rita answered. "He keeps me too busy to be lonesome while the rest of the family is at work. Rascal is so interesting. He washes his hands at the bathroom sink, but he has never learned to hang up a towel yet. He swims in the tub, opens the door when he wants to come in, and he even washes his food before he eats it. He is very clean."

"He has to wash his food," Irene said.

"What do you mean?" asked Rita.

"I just read an interesting article about raccoons in the Wildlife Magazine," Irene replied. "It said that raccoons have to put everything in water before they eat it. They don't have saliva glands in their mouth like other animals to help them chew their food. If they put something dry in their mouth and try to eat it, they can choke to death."

"Oh no! I didn't know that!" Rita exclaimed. "I just thought he was trying to be extra clean." Rita picked up Rascal and gave him a hug. She could not think about Rascal choking to death.

"Thanks for the coffee. I have a lot of shopping to do today, so I need to hurry to town a start buying groceries for my family," said Irene.

"Thanks for the information," Rita said, "I'm glad Rascal learned to wash his food before he choked to death. Rascal has never seen another raccoon and he has had to learn everything by him self. He really thinks he is a people person. I don't think he knows he is a raccoon."

"Animals do a lot of things through instinct and don't have to be trained. Maybe Rascal has learned a lot of things that way," Irene explained as Rita walked her to out to her car.

Rita watched her friend drive away before she put on her old clothes. She went outside and dug some of the ground in the brick planter by the front door and planted some more petunias. "I would not dare plant flowers in the back yard because the kids would destroy the flowers when they are playing football, basketball and waiting to jump on the trampoline," Rita told Rascal while he was also digging into the dirt.

Rascal weighed about thirty pounds now. Every day he tore up more things around the house. He pulled up Rita's large house plants in the dining room, and destroyed plants in the other rooms. Rascal crawled under the covers on the beds after Rita had made them. The beds were always messed up. He was always dumping out drawers and boxes. Rascal could jump up on the cabinets easily. It was impossible to put donuts and cookies out of his reach. A few times he had "accidents" when he backed up to the dining room wall. The rug showed where Rita had cleaned up the messes.

Rita was tired from all the extra work. It was enough work just to keep house for her family.

Rascal was now an adult. He grew more and more restless. Every night he crawled up the back of Pam's chair and kissed her on the cheek. Then sometimes he ran up the back of Ray Brown's chair and bite him on the neck and head while Ray was trying to watch TV.

One night Rascal jumped on Ray's head just as the telephone rang. It was one of his important customers. The man wanted irrigation well.

Ray tried to protect himself. He calmly told the man on the telephone, "Please excuse me and let me call you because a raccoon is attacking me." Ray tried to talk and looked dignified as he tried to protect himself from Rascal's attack. He looked so funny that Rita and the boys started laughing and couldn't stop laughing for a long time.

"Your customer probably thinks we have chickens in our house too," Rita said laughing. "They are probably wondering what kind of a place we live in."

It would soon be time for school to start again. Rita helped her sons buy school clothes and gym shoes. She bought new clothes for herself. Ronny started football practice two weeks before school started.

The first day of school was always busy. The students had to be enrolled. Grade books made ready and lesson plans for the next few days besides classes to teach. Rita came home from school tired and was ready to rest. She felt like crying when she walked into the house. Rascal had messed up every room in the house.

"Danny, Rascal has just grown too large to stay in the house any longer," Rita said with a sigh. "I think it is time to make him stay outside with Mickey."

"But, Mom, I'm afraid that something might happen to him outside," Danny replied.

"Rascal is plenty capable of taking care of himself," Rita said. "I think he would be happier outside with Mickey, anyway."

"What if he runs away and doesn't come back?" Danny asked. It made him feel sick to think what life would be like without Rascal.

"If he runs away, then it will be for the best," Rita answered. "I love him as much as you do, but he has never even seen another raccoon. Maybe he needs a family of his own. Maybe we are selfish for keeping him here."

"I guess he is too large to stay in the house, but I'll sure miss him if he leaves," said Danny.

"I will too, but I can't keep up with everything and all the messes he makes," Rita said.

Rascal became an outside raccoon.

Rita was watching the students at noon recess a week later. She saw a man walking toward her. Rita did not know the man. The man walked up to Rita.

"I'm Mr. Dewiest," the man said. "I hear that you have a raccoon at your place."

"Yes we do," Rita answered.

"Mrs. Brown, do you know it is against the law to have a raccoon penned up because they are protected by our government?" the man asked.

"But, he isn't penned up!" Rita exclaimed.

"What do mean that he isn't penned up?" the man asked.

"We turned him loose since he is big enough to take care of himself," Rita explained. "He has never been penned up."

"You mean you have had him in your house?" Mr. Dewiest asked.

"Yes, until a week ago when we started locking our doors so he can't get in at night, or when we are gone," Rita explained.

"Then where is he now?" Mr. Dewiest asked.

"In or around our yard," Rita answered.

"You mean that instead of putting him in a pen you have him tied up somewhere?" Mr. Dewiest asked.

"No!" Rita shouted. "We really turned him loose and he just likes to stay around us."

"Woman, do you expect me to believe that!" Mr. Dewiest shouted.

Rita was angry. "What I'm telling you is true!" she shouted. "We are the only family Rascal knows. If you don't believe me you can ask our neighbors. We have never tied up Rascal and he has never been penned up either."

"Okay Mrs. Brown. I guess I believe you," Mr. Dewiest said. He smiled and turned around to leave. He stopped and faced Rita again. "Don't forget that there is a law to protect raccoons. If I had found him penned up or tied up you would have too pay an eight-hundred dollar fine."

"I won't forget," Rita said. She sighed with relief while she watched Mr. Dewiest walk out of the school yard. "That would have been a lot of money to have to pay for Rascal," she Rita said to herself.

On Monday evening Rascal was not in the yard when Rita came home from work. Danny looked everywhere for him. "I told you he would run away," said Danny.

"I have the feeling that he will be back soon," Rita said.

"What if doesn't come back?" Danny asked.

"Then he will probably come back next spring with a family," Rita said with a smile.

"Cool," Danny said. "Do you really think so mom?" he asked.

"Oh dear. What would we do with two or three little Rascals to take care of?" Rita asked with a frown.

Danny looked for Rascal Tuesday evening. He looked all over town. He felt sad until he remembered what his mother had said. "It would be fun to have a house full of little Rascals," Danny was thinking.

Danny looked for Rascal again Wednesday as soon as he left school. He came back to the house. "Mom, I can't find Rascal anywhere," Danny said. "Granddad wanted me to help him at the shop this evening. I'll ride my motorcycle down there and be back before supper time."

"All right. Don't be sad son. I'm sure your friend will come back home and we will all be laughing again," Rita replied.

Rita decided to soak in the bathtub before she started supper. She felt tired and knew a warm bath would make her feel more rested. Rita put her best smelling bubble bath in the tub and was getting ready to relax in the warm water. As she was stepping into the tub, she heard something at the front door. She was happy because she knew it was Rascal. She heard the front door open. As she listened, the bathroom door flew open. There stood a large furry raccoon.

"Rascal, I'm so glad to see you!" Rita exclaimed. She reached out to pet Rascal. Rascal did not even look at Rita. He took one long dive and landed in the middle of the tub. Bubbles flew everywhere. Rascal made a couple of rounds in the bubbles for a few seconds before he jumped out and ran through every room in the house.

Rita put on her bathrobe. She was too busy wiping up bubbles from the carpet and floor to have time to take a bath. "I guess you took the bath for me you little rascal but I wish you would learn to dry off when you get out of the tub but I'm still glad to see you," Rita said as she was mopping up the floor.

Rascal spent the evening with the Brown family. Danny put him outside at bedtime and locked the door. They did not want to pay an eight-hundred dollar fine for keeping Rascal penned up.

The next evening Rascal was not in the yard when Danny and Rita came in after school. "I hope he hasn't run away again," Danny said. He looked for Rascal before he went to help his grandfather in the shop.

The Browns were watching TV that night. "Turn off the TV and listen," Rita told Ray.

The family smiled while they listened to Rascal open the front storm door and the front door. Rascal came running into the family room. He crawled up on Ronny's lap and pulled a pencil out of Ronny's shirt pocket. Ronny laughed when Rascal tried to write with it.

"Come here Rascal," Danny said. He was lying on the floor in front of the TV.

Rascal ran over to Danny and tried to chew on his ears. Danny and Rascal wrestled until Rascal grew tried. Rascal ran over to Ray's chair. He ran up the back of the chair and tried to chew on Ray's neck. Rascal pestered Ray Brown for a few minutes before he ran up the back of the couch.

Rita was lying on her stomach on the couch. Rascal jumped on her back and gave her a kiss on the cheek. He snuggled into a furry ball on the back of Rita's bare feet. Rascal slept there until it was time for everyone to go to bed.

Danny carried Rascal outside. "Goodnight Rascal and please don't run away again," he said. Rascal curled up beside Mickey on the front porch and both animals went to sleep.

Chapter IX

Who Knows?

Rascal did not run away again. Every evening the Browns heard him open the front door and come into the family room. "I wonder where he goes during the day?" Danny asked.

"He might have found an irrigation ditch close to town," Rita said. "You know how much he loves water.

It was Halloween. All the classes at school had scary parties. Most of the students were dressed in scary costumes and some strange things to eat were served at the parties. One mother brought a dark chocolate cake that was crumbled to look like dirt. The cake was in a flower pot with plastic flowers stuck in it. When the cake was served, the students squealed. There were gummy worms in the cake.

At first the students were not sure they wanted to eat the cake, but it was good and every one liked the gummy worms.

Another mother brought some powder sugar covered cereal in a dog food bag. The students had to be convinced that the goodies were not dog food before they would eat it. It was good too.

Rita and Danny hurried home from school and poured several packages of candy into large bowls. They put the bowls on the kitchen table. It wasn't long before the first group of "Trick or Treaters" came up the driveway and to the front door. Some looked like witches, some looked like black cats, and one child had a skeleton suit on.

Rascal saw the kids and smelled something sweet to eat. He made one long jump and landed on the planter next to the front door.

The children screamed and ran.

Rita heard the door bell ringing. By the time she was able to answer the door, she could hear the children screaming and running down the driveway.

"I think it was a bat!" one child was screaming.

Rita did not see anyone but Rascal. "What happened to our little visitors?" she asked.

Rascal just turned his head from side to side the way he always did when he was trying to figure out something.

"I think I better put you in the house before the next Trick and Treaters come to the door so you won't scare them." Rita said. She picked up Rascal and turned him loose in the house.

Rascal followed Rita into the kitchen.

Soon the door bell rang again. Rita invited the children into the kitchen. She held out the bowls of candy for them to take the pieces of candy they wanted.

"What is that!" one child dressed like a ghost exclaimed when Rascal waddled into the room.

"This is our pet raccoon, Rascal," Danny answered.

"Does he bite?" a child with a mask asked.

"Not usually," Rita answered. "Come here Rascal and let the children pet you." She picked Rascal up from the floor in order for the children to pet him. Rascal reached over and started taking candy out of the children's sacks.

"I'll be glad to share my candy with you," several children said. Each child let Rascal take a piece of candy from their sack.

"Rascal just loves sweets," Rita explained. "That's enough candy, Rascal, or you will be sick," She said when Rascal reached for more.

The rest of the evening was spent handing out candy, letting Rascal take a piece from each sack, and Rita putting the candy back in the children's sacks. Rascal enjoyed all the attention the children gave him.

Rita took care of the Treat or Treaters while she fixed supper. After Ronny finished eating he hurried back to school. His senior class was putting on a Halloween Carnival to raise money for a senior trip. Rita finished handing out the candy and cleaned up the kitchen.

"Are you ready to go to the carnival?" Ray asked.

"I don't think we will have any more visitors," Rita answered. "I guess I'm ready but I think we should leave Rascal in the house until we get back. I just hope he doesn't tear up anything while we are gone."

Danny crawled into the back seat. Ray and Rita crawled into the front seat of the family car. They were soon at the high school.

The seniors had set up everything they could think of to scare the kids and adults. There was an open grave where one of the senior boys rose up out of a coffin and talked to people. The student had his face painted white and his lips painted black. He looked so awful that no one could guess who it was.

There was a dark room where terrible noises were heard and objects grabbed at people.

The class had put up a fenced off area that they called their jail. People paid to have their friends, parents, or teachers "arrested". The people in the jail had to pay to get out.

The seniors were making a lot of money for their trip. They were planning to spend a few days next summer in Branson, Missouri and visit the Ozark country.

Danny paid to have his father and mother put in jail. They had to pay two dollars each to get out. Several times Rita's students paid to have her put in jail. Rita had to pay to get out each time. She was glad that her money was going to a good cause.

It was late when Danny and his parents came home. They were tired and went right to bed after Rascal was let out.

The carnival was over. It was almost midnight by the time the seniors cleaned up the mess in the school rooms. "May I take you home?" Ronny asked his girlfriend.

"Yes," Alan's sister answered. "My folks went home a long time ago."

"Let's drive out to the mile corner south of town before I take you home," Ronny suggested.

"That sounds all right to me," Kim replied. "I'm too tired to be sleepy right now anyway."

Ronny and Kim saw car lights coming toward them. The car swerved partly into the ditch. "I wonder what they are doing?" Ronny asked.

Ronny and Kim both groaned as they saw a raccoon lying in the ditch beside the road. It had been hit by the car.

Ronny stopped the car and got out to look at the dead raccoon. It was too dark to tell if it was Rascal or not. "Whoever did it had to go off the road to hit him," Ronny said. "They hit him just for the fun of it."

"I just hope it isn't Rascal," Kim said.

"I do too. It would be hard for Danny to lose Rascal," Ronny replied. "I would miss him too."

Ronny took Kim home. Neither one felt like talking. They were thinking that it probably was Rascal.

The next morning Ronny told Danny about the raccoon. "I don't think it was big enough to be Rascal," Ronny said.

"I'm sure it wasn't Rascal," Danny replied. "He is too smart to get run over by a car. I'm going to go outside and look for him right now." He left the house and crawled on his motorcycle.

Ronny watched Danny ride away. "I just couldn't tell Danny but I think it was Rascal that we saw last night," he told Rita. "I don't know of any other raccoon that would be that close to town." "I sure hope it wasn't him," Ronny said.

Danny looked all over town and called for Rascal in every area. "I know Rascal is still alive somewhere," he told himself over and over. He did not want to lose all hope by checking the carcass south of town.

It was late at night when Ray Brown woke up. Rita was not in bed. He looked at the clock. It said 3:30. The bathroom light was on. "Rita must be sick," Ray said. He got up and knocked on the bathroom door. "Rita, are you sick?" Ray asked.

"No," Rita answered.

"Then what is the matter with you?" Ray asked.

"I'm just crying over a silly raccoon," Rita sobbed.

"I'll miss him to," said Ray.

"Rascal is not dead," Danny said at breakfast the next morning. "He has just gone somewhere to find him a girl raccoon. He will come back to us in the spring with a family of his own just like you said he would mom. Someday he will open the front door and come in like he always did. He will introduce our family to his family. You just wait and see."

Danny looked for Rascal every evening until the snow started to fall. "Rascal is hibernating somewhere now," he said. He stopped looking for Rascal and tried to get interested in basketball.

The next spring Rita, Danny, and Velvet went to the creek many times to hunt for raccoons. Maybe they were just looking for one special raccoon.

Whenever Velvet smelled the raccoon tracks around the water holes she would bounce around happily. She thought that she was going to see Rascal again. And, maybe she will, someday. Who knows?

The Browns were thankful to God that they were blessed to have had a pet raccoon like Rascal.